Detached Y

Mission at the Margins

Steve Blower

Youth Project Manager

Sidewalk Youth Organization, Scarborough

GROVE BOOKS LIMITED

RIDLEY HALL RD CAMBRIDGE CB3 9HU

Contents

Dedication
For Anna, Theo and Madeleine.

First Impression June 2020
ISSN 1748-3492
ISBN 978 1 78827 127 1

1

Introduction

> Exquisite mutuality at the margins.[1]

Detached youth work, rooted in the Christian tradition, can be a great way of connecting with and supporting socially excluded young people. But it can be more than that. Fr Gregory Boyle suggests, 'We don't go to the margins to make a difference. We go to the margins so that folks at the margins make *us* different.'[2] Approached with humility, critical awareness and creativity, detached work is a participation in the transformative good news as it is discovered in collaboration with those on the margins.

Jon Sobrino says salvation comes from below. 'It is the poor who will save the world.'[3] How strange. It is almost as though God chose the weak, the poor, the lowly and the despised to turn things upside down! This is not some vengeful act of retribution against the rich and powerful. It is rather a recognition that things can often be seen more clearly from the outside, the margins. Jesus spent most of his time with outsiders, rejects, the stigmatized, who went on to become his body, the church.

I have been involved in youth work for twenty years. Most of that time has been spent at churches or youth centres, but a few years ago I joined Sidewalk, an ecumenical detached youth project. In this work I discovered something that I had sensed deep down the whole time. My very first experience of detached youth work, shadowing the project leader, made a real impression.

> Conversations during the evening were candid, challenging and real. At one location I observed the worker engaging with a young person who just had a fight with a group of exchange students from France. He said that they looked like terrorists.
>
> The interaction progressed into an exploration of identity, media, diversity and community.

I was struck by the rapport and open dialogue with young people who did not attend groups or clubs. In the years since, I have found this to be the new normal. Detached youth work meets young people, who are often socially excluded, where they are at. In doing so it creates space to learn what things look like from the edge, and negotiate from that place what positive transformation and good news might look like.

This booklet has been arranged loosely around Kolb's learning cycle. Chapter two will look at what detached youth work is and provide an example in practice. In chapters three and four we will reflect on this and draw on wider theory to expand a bit on how the Christian tradition brings valuable insight and values to the practice. Chapter five will then outline a framework for the development of a faith-based detached youth work project. Then it is over to the reader; see you on the streets!

What is Detached Youth Work? 2

We're not the fourth emergency service.[4]

The 'Unclubbables'

Youth clubs and centres in the community are great resources that can provide warmth, shelter, safety and space for young people to gather. Why leave this behind and engage in detached work? Is not youth work about getting young people *off* the streets?![5]

I remember visiting a church-based youth club I had been invited to volunteer at. They were keen to connect positively with local young people.

It was mayhem and, as an onlooker, quite exciting! But as I watched, I felt the struggle of the volunteer team who were scrambling to maintain safety in the environment they had set up for the 30 or so young people. They rushed around, anxiously trying to persuade young visitors to refrain from fighting, launching pool balls, smoking, etching graffiti into furniture and playing music on the sound system that would have raised eyebrows on a Sunday morning!

Afterwards, the team agreed how important it was to provide space for the young people, but expressed despair at how difficult it was to police the environment and its attendees. As time went on, more rigorous rules were enforced and the whole space began to feel more calm, safe and manageable. Some young people adapted. Others left.

The shift in atmosphere at the youth club was a welcome one but a kind of spark had vanished, along with a number of young people with whom the team had been keen to work.

Beyond the Building

The centre-based work continued to prove popular with lots of young people and developed a creative discipleship programme that I enjoyed being part of. But what about those who had left? They had not disappeared. Those young people were still around. They just were not at the club!

We had done all we could to help them, right? If they did not appreciate it and ruined it for other people then what could we do about it? Some years later I found an approach to work that 'focuses on engaging young people who are not accessing services, particularly when barriers exist to their participation.'[6] I had discovered detached youth work.

History

Detached work arguably emerged in the late 1950s as a distinctive youth work practice. It emerged out of a cultural context of moral panic, investment in youth services and the aim of engaging unattached young people who were not accessing mainstream services. The Albemarle Report highlighted that 'Some [young people] are too wary or too deeply estranged to accept, at any rate initially, even the slight commitment required by club membership.' It went on to suggest the need for 'peripatetic youth workers, not attached directly to any organization or premises, who would work with existing groups or gangs of young people.'[7]

In the 1960s and 1970s detached work became a mainstay of youth provision. In the 1980s and 1990s funding and social policy increasingly influenced its practice and priorities. Gradually the work became host to various agendas like truancy, teenage pregnancy, drugs and public safety. Detached youth work values and practice were strained by these factors. More recently, the shrinking of the state, austerity and target-driven funding programmes have presented additional challenges. Despite this, the practice continues to offer unique and valuable contributions within a diminished youth sector.

Whilst historically, this approach has been used widely through statutory services, the potential of detached work as youth ministry is huge. Over the past twenty years, innovative approaches to mission have emerged through StreetSpace, now known as Frontier Youth Trust. FYT continues to provide a network for such projects and a context for theological reflection on detached youth work.[8]

Definitions

The term 'detached' is used to describe youth workers who operate beyond the formal structures and environments that other forms of youth work take place in. We will see how 'The boundaries of centre-based work are drawn much more tightly than for detached work.'[9]

Karen Malone writes about youth culture in public spaces and her insights help to distinguish further detached work from other forms of youth work.[10] I have gathered some of her observations (shaded) alongside those of Sidewalk's detached youth work practitioners in the table below:

Characteristic	Detached work	Centre-based work
Definition of boundary	Fluid	Clear and defined
Value system	Multiple values supported	Dominant values normalized
Response to difference	Celebrated	Tolerated to a degree
Role of policing	Policing of boundaries not necessary	Preoccupation with boundary maintenance, high level of policing
View of culture	Multicultural	Monocultural
Power	Negotiated	Contested
Engages with	Marginalized	Socialized
Context	Set by young people	Set by organization

For some young people the question of detached youth work or centre-based youth work is redundant because they simply would not spend their own time in a space that is monitored by adults.

> We spoke to Jim in the football cage one evening and he said, 'The local youth club is shit, you have to scan your hand to get in and it's for kids anyway.'

But detached work is not simply valued for its capacity to reach young people who may not feel comfortable in more structured environments. It 'endeavours to provide a broad-based, open-ended, social education in which the problems and issues to be dealt with, and the manner in which they are dealt with, emerges from dialogue between the young person and the youth worker.'[11]

So, whilst detached youth work is frequently understood in terms of *where* it happens, there are equally factors that shape *how* it happens. In a distinct way, detached youth work seems to embed values of mutuality, democracy and negotiation in the process of social education.

Because of the looser connection with established structures and systems there is also a significant degree of improvisation with detached work. Detached youth workers 'celebrate the uncertainty implied by an open-ended way of working' whereby they participate with young people in shaping the agenda, context and terms of engagement.[12]

For these reasons detached youth work is considered distinct from outreach, whereby a youth project will seek to draw young people back into a youth centre in order to deliver prescribed work. It is also distinct from mobile youth work, which involves a vehicle or outreach mechanism effectively enabling a youth centre to move to where young people are. Neither one is better than the other, but the aims and approaches of both are distinct.

Power and Agenda

Although in public, detached youth work does not take place in neutral spaces, nor is it done with agenda-free participants. In terms of power, authority and agenda, 'What sets detached youth work apart is its willingness to negotiate on these issues and on *where* it takes place…the agenda must emerge from a mutually respectful relationship.'[13] In Scarborough, young people at Hairybob's Skatepark have observed that the facility was built well away from the town, as though it was intended to keep them out of sight and away from public life. I often hear encouragements from members of the community praising youth work organizations in terms of how they 'get kids off the streets.' David Sibley highlights some of the underlying factors that make public spaces more or less hostile to certain groups, including young people.[14]

Awareness of these factors is valuable to detached work where 'The nature of the physical spaces we enter sets the tone for the interactions that follow.'[15] We have already considered the impact of environment on young people and those who work with them. When young people are at home, school, church, youth groups and in other structured environments there are established norms and enforced expectations.

When young people are in structured environments there are established norms

In a subtler way, this applies to public spaces too. But when on the streets, under bridges, in parks and public spaces young people are often consciously positioning themselves apart from environments in which behaviours are so closely monitored and norms rigorously enforced. For young people, then, public spaces can represent a context of anti-structure where they can explore their own values. We will pick up on this theme later on.

The Joseph Rowntree Foundation reports that, 'Public spaces are a particular and distinct resource for young people looking to socialize with others. However, groups of young people are sometimes perceived as having antisocial intentions, which in many cases is simply not true.'[16] On the flip side, when a detached youth work team turns up where young people are gathered in this context there is usually at least a hint of suspicion among the young people that an adult group has come to monitor their behaviour. 'Who do you work for?…Are you feds?' Given that this environment is the one in which many young people can most fully express their otherness in relation to the structures within which they live, such concerns are understandable.

Do not Take a Purse or Bag or Sandals or Pool Table...

Luke writes that when Jesus sends out disciples ahead of him, they are to go as guests, without resources, dependent on those they meet. This sets up an important host / guest dynamic that ensures that those taking good news with them are ready also to be recipients of good news among those they meet.

When we are out and about on the streets, we do not have games consoles, tuck shops, pool tables and all the other resources associated with youth provision. Instead, we bring our own inquisitive dispositions and positive regard in search of the light that is already there, ready, in the words of George Fox, to answer that of God in everyone.

Detached work is about stepping beyond our spaces of control and into public spaces, mutually shared, but inhabited first by young people.

Example

In 2016 I joined Sidewalk, a Christian detached youth project based in the North Yorkshire coastal town of Scarborough. It has been delivering this kind of work since the 1980s when it was set up by a group of churches to connect with socially excluded young people in the town.

Two members of the Sidewalk detached team arrive at the children's play area of a local park on a cold dark winter's night. A couple of young people are swinging around on monkey bars while another dashes up the side of a flyover bridge and jumps off to the tarmac below. The scene presents as a bit chaotic. We sit down nearby and take some hot chocolate from our kit bag. They come to see what we are up to, share a drink and we start to chat.

'We're working out,' one of them says.

'Why?'

'We get really angry; we need somewhere to put it, and we want to get fit.'

Two of the three had been excluded from school, the other was struggling to settle in after his family had been relocated from another part of the country. One team member highlights how inspiring their actions are and asks if there is any way Sidewalk can join in. They talk about wanting somewhere proper to train.

Later that week, the workers accompany the young people to a local gym. The gym manager listens to the young people and responds by providing support and space for them to work out—On Mondays, they can even train with a professional boxer! Now these young people have resources to develop what they had been doing in the park.

A month or so later one of the workers is chatting with one of the young people. 'I didn't like gyms before I came here. You got this thing started and, do you know what, I'm actually getting a lot out of it. Thanks!'

The young person, ordinarily stone faced, lets slip a grin. He gained more from being the creator of a service than simply a beneficiary.

As the months go on, the core group invites others who are struggling with bereavement, body image, bullying, anxiety, depression and other challenges. A year later the project has benefited a dozen other young people and spawned other projects including fund-raisers and bike rides.

This example is a particularly positive one. Most of the time, there is not such an immediate connection between conversation and practical action. But it does highlight the kind of impact detached youth work values can have in practice. Mutuality, negotiated agendas, open-ended working and improvisation are all present. It also demonstrates a strength-based approach that we will turn to next.

That of God

3

> If I really believe that in every person I meet there is 'that of God,' what a difference it makes![17]

In the next two chapters we will explore social theory and theology to reflect further on detached youth work. First, then, we briefly consider the use of strength-based approaches in youth work and ministry.

Scarcity and Abundance

I was schooled in needs-based approaches to youth work. The most commonly used tool for this was probably the NAOMIE framework, which takes as its starting point the identification of needs.[18] All the subsequent stages are then built on this foundation of deficit relief. In a way, this approach starts with less than nothing. It tends to focus attention on issues, problems and weakness. A few years ago, some young people made me aware of a different way of approaching things.

> We went paintballing with a group of young people. After a morning of shooting at each other I went to pick up our pre-ordered pizzas. I brought them back to the group, handed them round and when I got to the last person, there was no pizza. I had counted wrong. The lad looked at me and said, 'It's ok.' His deflated demeanour and the contour of his eyebrows suggested otherwise! I rushed off to order another pizza before the afternoon paintball session began.
>
> By the time I had got back it was too late. They were all sat around laughing, chatting and comparing bruises from the morning session and when I offered the pizza to the young person he shrugged and said he didn't want it.
>
> 'Why' I asked.
>
> 'Everyone's given me a slice of theirs; you keep it.'
>
> They all ate and were satisfied.

I had seen only need. The young people saw something else—the resources already available: their communal spirit and an abundance of pizza! I reflected on how the role of provider in that situation had shifted from me, the youth worker, to the young people. I was so busy trying to address the need that it had not even crossed my mind that the young people already had it covered. The young people perceived sufficiency, what Brueggemann calls a manna-based culture.[19] Meanwhile, my messiah complex was dented!

It raised broader questions about my ideas and attitudes regarding youth work, young people and mission. The church I was working with at the time provided lots of great programmes and activities for young people, but I could see that these young people were more than able to lead the way for themselves. Were we contributing to the barriers they faced by controlling and extending a narrative of deficit?

It is Easy as ABC…D

I later discovered *asset-based community development* (ABCD), which helped further the language and understanding that would enable us more or less to flip our needs-based approach on its head. The premise of ABCD is that 'Communities can drive the development process themselves by identifying and mobilizing existing, but often unrecognized assets.'[20] Asset-based approaches do not replace needs-based work. They go hand in hand. It is just that it begins by saying, 'This community already has stuff to use in pursuit of its dreams.' At Sidewalk we talk about being asset-based and deficit-conscious.

Youth work can be creative, collaborative and generative rather than a preventative service

So, rather than just seeing youth work as a preventative service, it can be creative, collaborative and generative beyond just meeting the needs of those engaged with it. The case study of the gym group in the previous chapter suggests there is value in such a process. As Malone points out, 'Youth have different cultural values, understandings and needs—differences that should be supported and valued as significant contributions to the social capital of cities and towns.'[21]

Within Sidewalk, organizational and staff perceptions regarding young people and the community have balanced some of the negative assumptions of need with more positive regard and awareness of inherent capacity. Young people also seem more likely to self-identify as active co-creators than passive recipients of services.

The idea of young people 'Hanging around in groups on street corners, talking, playing or simply observing others is viewed as inappropriate.'[22] This picture is often associated with concerns of antisocial behaviour. On the flip side, it also presents as uncomfortably prosocial behaviour within such a fragmented and individualized society. If young people develop community practices in public spaces, could we not be watching, learning, joining in?!

Manna-culture

Young people's natural ability to find new ways of thinking and being in community is addressed by Jesus too. Looking at John's account of the feeding of the five thousand (John 6), a boy is identified who comes forward offering, not pizza this time, but bread and fish. Whilst others are wondering how they will finance such a grand feast (the deficit outlook), the boy starts with what he already has. Jesus receives this and blesses it. Those with whom we work are often already participating in a countercultural narrative that aligns with and contributes to the *missio Dei.*

Mission Monopoly

I grew up with an idea of mission as being about taking God's light into darkness. Sure, detached youth work often happens in darkness, but we usually find light already very much present when meeting young people out and about. Christians do not have a monopoly on light! We are all made in the image of God and have divine riches to share. Rowan Williams highlights the now popular description of mission as 'finding out what God is doing and joining in.'[23] Detached youth work can be enriched with this idea that God is already at work in the spaces we visit, and our role is to participate.

Youth ministry can bring a reverence and respect for young people that is transformational for the workers, young people and the wider community. The transformation can even lead to roles being blurred and flipped. This is similar to Freire's suggestion that the teacher is a student and the student a teacher where both are 'jointly responsible for a process in which all grow.'[24] The Quaker tradition speaks about addressing that of God in everyone. Doncaster suggests, 'If there really is that of God in every man, then every man may be a channel through whom God may be better known to us.'[25] It works both ways.

Faith-based detached youth work brings, 'deep reverence for human personality' and 'faith in the potentialities that may not be immediately visible.'[26] We are participating in God's mission when we connect with that of God in the other.

4 Liminality—Mission from the Margins

Liminality is the ultimate teachable space.[27]

Betwixt and Between!

We have explored a bit about what makes detached youth work unique and valuable as well as how Christian theology resonates with the practice. Now we will explore liminality, an idea that I believe frames detached youth work as a transformative resource for young people and their communities.

What is Liminality?

Liminality is a term that comes from the Latin, *limen*, meaning threshold. A threshold is that space between two places. It is neither here nor there; it is in-between. Anthropologist Victor Turner talked about rites of passage as being important thresholds for members of a community to transition from one life stage to another.[28]

Rites of passage for a number of societies and tribes involve being excluded from the community before being reintegrated as a changed person. Turner describes the in-between phase as a 'liminal state.' There are parallels here with the Christian tradition of baptism. So, too, we can read Jesus' wilderness experience as a liminal experience. He leaves the community and spends forty gruelling days of challenge and isolation before returning with clarity of vision and purpose that will bring lasting change among a new community. The motif of wilderness frequently seems to be accompanied by a challenging in-between space that marks significant transformation. Moses' exile was the vehicle for his calling and Israel's desert experience gave rise to their new community. The spaces in which detached youth workers meet young people are also charged with these qualities of discomfort and transformation.

There is a lot about detached youth work that can be understood as liminal. Young people, as adolescents, are ambiguously caught between clearer socially defined categories of child and adult. The outdoor spaces young people use are often between other places, under bridges, paths, corners, streets and so on. Even street-based youth workers are liminal in that they have partially detached themselves from structural apparel and association.

In this chapter, we will focus on how liminality might affect young people and inform detached youth work practice. I will use the theory to suggest young people experiencing marginalization have intrinsic and unique capacities to address wider structural issues.

To do this we need to explore what liminality does. Sang Hyun Le, theologian and pastor of a marginal Asian-American community in the USA, makes some interesting observations and identifies Jesus as a model of liminality.[29] Below is my adaptation of his ideas as they apply to detached youth work (see also Figure 1, p 19).

Chaos

This first stage highlights the separation of a person from the established social structures and relationships maintained by their community. Liminality has a close relationship with marginality. Whether excluded by choice, requirement or structural issues, the experience of liminality is challenging yet potentially transformational. Jesus was familiar with this position; as a Galilean Jew under Roman occupation he was on the margins of the margins. His ministry is inaugurated in the wilderness by John the Baptist.

Detached youth work aims to connect with those young people on the margins of structures like school, family or community. As with the outsiders in Jesus' time, young people today often have critical perspectives on aspects of community life and structures about which they have had negative experiences.

The young people and the youth workers are both, to an extent, liminal parties engaging on the margins of broader social structures and systems. Workers must be able to communicate their aims clearly as they may otherwise simply be viewed as part of a dominant structure that young people are on the streets often specifically to avoid.

Part of this process involves supporting and nurturing young people's ability to see and analyze things critically from the outside. Detached youth workers should be open to the unknown potential of meeting young people where they are at. This often means refraining from judgment in the face of what may be dismissed and condemned as challenging behaviour. This does not mean the absence of critical engagement, only that the role of the detached youth worker is one of empathy and dialogue, instead of judgment and sanction.

Communitas

This stage sees the formation of new relationships among other marginalized people where experiences and values are shared. Turner describes *communitas* as a way of relating to others without the hierarchies, social roles, expectations and limitations getting in the way.[30] Through this process, alternative practices and values can emerge.

Jesus clearly spent time developing relationships with social outcasts and fostering alternative community. Tax collectors, prostitutes, lepers, Samaritans, terrorists, criminals and others shared a common low status in the social hierarchies of the day and started to form connections around the more hopeful values and practices that Jesus shared.

Young people connect with each other differently outside of social structures

In a similar way, young people connect with each other differently outside of social structures. New relationships develop in which values and practices emerge that are divergent from dominant social norms. From my experience of detached work, it is quite common to see groups of young people interacting with a shared alternative moral and social code. 'Those who are marginalized…can use their marginality as an opportunity for radical possibility…a new reality can be envisaged, construed and lived.'[31] Skatepark communities often have their own values and practices that are shaped by those who use them. This emerges from shared marginality and the desire to shape ways of being human that are integral to their experience and values rather than those imposed upon them.

When detached workers build positive relationships with young people at this stage, the environment is energized with potential. The worker can be an ally in the process. Exploring alternative values and practices with young people creates a rich context for social and informal education as ideas, possibilities and hopes are nurtured.

Creativity

In this third stage, marginalized people return to the established structures with new insight, critique and ideas to challenge established ideas and energize positive change. Here, new values and practices can be applied into the wider social context.

Jesus advocated an alternative way of living within the structures of his time that was both radical and effective. It was popular among the socially excluded, because it included and valued them. Conversely, it was broadly met with resistance from those of higher status, who had more to lose.

There are times when young people's critical voices and alternative values are dismissed or resisted. 'Why are the government so slow to address the climate crisis?' 'Why won't my teacher listen to me just like I listen to him?' 'Why should I study if there are no opportunities or good jobs around here?'

This stage has the capacity to elevate young people's concerns and issues, as detached youth workers can advocate on their behalf. But they can also foster the awareness, knowledge, skills and connections young people need to communicate their viewpoints directly to the right people in the most effective way. 'Young people often test the boundaries associated with the mores and norms of their local community and wider society. [Detached youth work] tries to offer a medium in which young people can do this positively.'[32]

If heard rather than told, nurtured rather than controlled, promoted rather than prevented, young people's critiques and alternative practices will flourish and positively impact the wider community

Liminal Youth Work in Practice

Applying this to the gospel narrative, Jesus leaves established structures behind, forms new community in the desert with John the Baptist and others, then challenges the flaws in established structures and promotes the practice of alternative values and ideas, often referred to as the kingdom of God.

Young people we meet in the parks and streets of Scarborough occupy in-between, wilderness spaces. Whilst here, they connect with one another and form *communitas*—new configurations of community, based on shared marginalization and the expression of alternative values. This solidarity and shared marginalization leads to a third stage of reconnecting with the established structures of community. Now, though, they bring a certain otherness with them. They are changed. Together they express a critique of the community that has led to their marginalization, but they also creatively present and enact their alternative values and practices.

Young people creatively present and enact their alternative values and practices

The gym group story provides a helpful example. We met the young people in an outdoor space where they shared with us about their frustrations including exclusion from school, and a lack of facilities (chaos). The young people gathered in solidarity, forming new social relationships and community based on their shared values, interests and practices (*communitas*). The young people then created a community-based group that facilitated other marginalized young people to thrive, grow and participate in ways that were meaningful to them (creativity).

It is not surprising that the young people who have had the greatest positive impact in the community where I work are the very ones who have experienced exclusion at school, rejection at home or other forms of marginalization.

That said, the aim of the framework is not to move young people through a prescriptive process. Not all groups will transition through the stages, nor should they be expected to. Rather, the three outlined stages give detached youth workers a way of understanding their work in a wider social context, and identifying appropriate opportunities for social education and transformation, both for the young people and the communities they are part of.

Turner suggests that liminality has an important role in facilitating communities to adapt and progress with inevitable changes.[33] If this is the case, then those on the margins should be valued and supported through the experience and, furthermore, should be heard and recognized as contributors to the shaping of a more hopeful future.

Detached youth work locates us with others in the wilderness, where solidarity and creativity emerge as catalysts for change, and the grassroots burst through with new life.

Questions for Reflection

- What is our role in the chaos, communitas and creativity young people experience?
- How can we champion the voice and action of marginalized young people towards new possibilities?

Liminal youth work

Exploring transformation from the margins

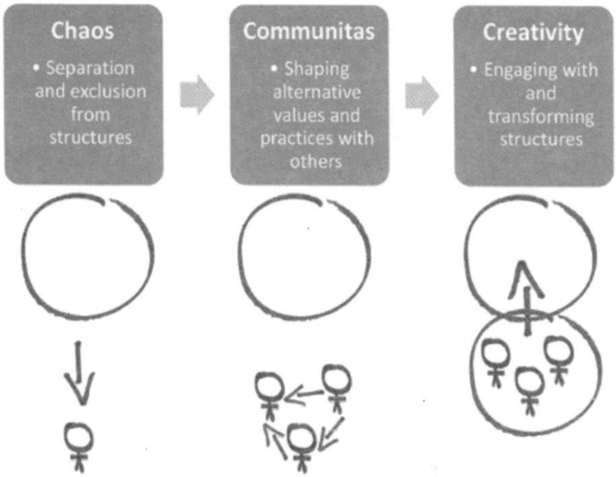

	Chaos	Communitas	Creativity
Signs	Disengagement Exclusion Marginalisation Withdrawal Uncertainty	Growth of confidence Discovery New thinking Experimentation Group identities emerge	Generative action Grassroots activism Challenging structures Struggle for change Community mobilization
Threats	Vulnerability Low confidence Risks to wellbeing	Cliques Negative culture External social control	Cultural assimilation Structural resistance Despair from lack of change
Opportunities	Freedom from structures Voice pain Conscientisation	Voice of hope Community Solidarity	Voice in action Transformative participation Benefit to yps & community
Youthwork practice	Trust Hope Solidarity Encouragement		
	Listening skills Empathy Safe space Validation Equal opportunity	Informal ed Challenge/explore values Groupwork Team building New experiences	Resources Skills development Mediation Platforming Championing

Sidewalk Youth Project

5 Tools for the Task

All real living is meeting.[34]

Having explored detached youth work and considered how the Christian tradition resonates with the practice, we will now take a step towards action and look at how things can be put into practice. This chapter presents a framework for getting started. The practice of detached youth work can broadly be broken down into four phases: preparation, contact, intervention and moving on.[35] That said, these are not necessarily linear, and work will have to adapt and be responsive to an evolving process.

Preparation

Key Considerations

Before developing a detached youth work project, it is important to consider:

- What current provision already exists in the area, and who is not accessing it?
- Who has determined a need for detached youth work, and why?
- What are the aims of developing detached youth work in your context?
- Is there sufficient finance, resource and capacity to support detached youth work, including training, supervision, resources, rent etc?
- Is there a base venue with resource to manage administration and store equipment?

Essentials

Detached youth work may simply look like a couple of people out and about wearing backpacks, but it is what goes on in the background that makes their work effective and safe. Below are some key considerations. Further practical information and support can be accessed through the FDYW (Federation for Detached Youth Work), see www.fdyw.org.uk.

- *Aims*—These should be clearly defined and communicated to all stakeholders. Do the aims of the project fit within an existing organization, or is the project a separate entity with its own governing document and structures?
- *Safety*—Appropriate policies and staff training will need to be developed for health and safety, safeguarding, risk assessments, emergency procedures and responses to risky behaviour and substance abuse.
- *Paperwork*—Similarly, other documents and policies including data and confidentiality, job descriptions, contracts, equality and diversity and codes of practice should be made. Appropriate insurance and enhanced DBS checks also need to be in place.
- *Kit*—You will need to consider what equipment to take out. ID cards showing organizational information, first aid kit, project mobile phone and appropriate clothing are all key. Other items should be considered according to the context: torches, personal alarms, information and flyers about available services, refreshments, conversation starters and ice breakers. Kit will need to be stored safely at a base venue.
- *Monitoring and evaluating*—Having a process in place to measure the effectiveness of the work is vital. A write-up form template tailored for detached sessions may include information about areas visited, numbers of young people seen, weather, learning points and challenges faced and other factors including the means to record how the aims of the project are being addressed. There may also be the need to measure outcomes for funders, so appropriate recording and measuring processes will need to be considered.
- *Finance*—One important aspect of a project's sustainability is finance. Funding can be sourced through local donations, statutory grants, trust funds or elsewhere, but consideration in the budget should be given to cover two staff per session, training, equipment, additional interventions and projects, supervision, monitoring, evaluating, base venue costs and an appropriate time scale for the project. A few months of funding leading to the provision and then quick withdrawal of a service can serve to do more harm than good. It is also important to consider the aims and agendas tied to any financial support, for reasons that were explored briefly earlier.

Local Knowledge and Planning

Before walking into a dark room, it makes sense to turn the light on. Then we can see how big the room is, what is there, and what is not there. In the same way, approaching detached youth work with our eyes open is important. Defining the geographical area to be covered, and what is in that area, will help to focus and inform work delivered. Creating a *community profile* is a valuable process, generating contextual understanding.[36] Data generated from a broad range of sources including photos, surveys, ONS data, local service information, council reports, local news, information about local schools and walking around the area at different times will help to build a picture of the local context and its socio-economic and political landscape. Consider both what is missing in the area, as well as the assets and resources.

The findings should be summarized in a research report which will inform the work that follows. The summarized report should be able to inform and present recommendations on the practical questions of what time to go out, how often, what areas to visit and what groups to engage with. Work on the community profile may well take up to six months, but will serve to ground the project with valuable understanding, awareness and sensitivity to the local context. This period is also the perfect time to provide training for the team. All workers will need an induction covering policies, procedures, training and a structure for ongoing support and supervision. If there is nobody on the team who has experience delivering detached youth work, it would certainly be worth factoring in some external training and support.

Initial Contact

Now you are ready to go! You have done the training and the research. You have got your kit bag, and you head out with your team mate. You see a group of young people ahead. This bit can seem scary! Even experienced detached youth workers will feel the uncertainty of engaging with a new group of young people. I would suggest three ways you can increase assurance and confidence in these situations. Being prepared, being yourself, and seeing that of God in the other.

You can be prepared by having an introduction ready. It should include your name, the organization you represent and what you are doing. You may have some flyers or social media links and information to share so the young people can clarify what you are doing, and also know how to get in touch to follow up. Authenticity is important to young people, so be yourself and anticipate an encounter with someone amazing—because they are! If the community profile has been going on over months, there is a good chance that the young people may have already noticed and become curious about your presence in the community. In my experience, sooner or later, the young people are likely to engage you in conversation rather than the other way around.

When initiating contact, nerves and a sense of expectation can prompt workers to over talk. It is helpful to see the initial contact phase as an opportunity to listen, discover and learn about what young people think of the area and the possibility of connecting with detached teams.

It is funny how something as small as a nod can genuinely foster a sense of success at this early stage! And remember, if a group does not want to engage, that is okay! They know you will be around if they want to connect and, more often than not, my experience has been, eventually they will. Voluntary participation is a core principle of youth work, and it is just the same with detached. Some further reading on this and the other phases in this chapter can be found in Richard and Lorimer Passmore's *Here Be Dragons*, a really helpful book on detached youth work from a faith perspective.[37]

Establishing and Developing Relationships

So, you have made contact. Now what? Getting to know young people is an ongoing process and will naturally develop through regular and reliable presence, trust, mutuality and respect. Developing rapport takes time. In addition, attentiveness to the group dynamics and culture will inform your approach. Who are the leaders in the group? Who are the quieter ones and how do they participate? Are there subgroups, or overlaps with other groups? Listening and learning about the concerns, interests, hopes, fears and ideas the young people have is essential. This will inform your understanding of their world and show that you care.

Developmental Work and Youth-led Action

Young people's views, concerns and interests become the content for social and informal education as actions are explored and implemented. It might be the formation of a planning group to run an event, a social media campaign, a trip or another action. Tiffany highlights a central tenet of youth work as 'supporting young people in becoming initiators, creators and developers of curriculum, shaped by critical dialogue.'[38] Effective social education emerges through the process of young people organizing and acting to address issues relevant to them.

Youth-led action is a dynamic process, and different groups will require different levels and types of support that need to be thoughtfully negotiated. Too little support may lead to frustrations and disengagement. On the other hand, too much support will diminish the capacity for social education and young people will have a reduced sense of investment and ownership. Research suggests, that 'Young people are rarely challenged to identify issues that are of interest to them, or helped to develop mechanisms to address these issues through their own actions.'[39]

There have been times when I have attempted to rescue a group struggling to implement actions, then seen engagement drop off in proportion to the increased intervention. We do not always get it right. Young people will not either. But that is ok. It is often failure that generates the deepest learning. In that sense, failure might then become a measure of success! The key is to be an ally and informal educator through the process with young people. Nothing is wasted, not even a failed idea.

Exploring Spirituality

Effective long-term rapport building and collaborative working is likely to lead to a greater sense of trust and connection between young people and the youth workers. This naturally tends towards deeper conversation, exploration and reflection. As young people are supported to reflect on their actions and interventions, the bigger life questions arise in context—'What's the point of doing a skate festival for others?' 'We're doing food packs, but why are there homeless people in the first place?' 'What does a better society look like?' 'Why do we have to fight so hard to be heard?'

Such explorations are a valuable extension of the informal education process. To use a Steve Bevans analogy, the workers are like treasure hunters who take a map to an unknown place and work with locals to decipher it and find the treasure.[40] This helps us to see spiritual exploration as a contextual and participative process.

Both the young people and the workers learn, as they explore together the meanings that arise and manifest in their context. The journey is one of mutual discovery, and so long as workers have been clear about any faith context that the work is set in, the contributions made will be understood within that frame of reference. FYT have created skatepark parables and street-corner stories which contextualize theology within young people's experience to explore deep questions.[41]

There may be a temptation to see this as the spiritual bit of the work. Whilst this stage can be of great value, it should not be used as some sort of 'God slot' or faith bolt-on. As we have explored throughout the booklet, faith-based detached youth work is charged with a spirituality of goodness (that of God in everyone), struggle (chaos), connectedness and growth (*communitas*), justice, hope and transformation (creativity). The whole process should be integrated and authentic.

Adapting to Changes

During this phase it is worth recognizing the fluid and changing context of life for young people and how this may affect the regularity and flow of ongoing work with a group. Things might be going brilliantly, but then they stop hanging out in the same spot. You might spot a group that you have not seen for months, and then find that they are keen to do something straight away. The voluntary nature of youth work brings with it an acceptance of the ebb and flow of focused engagement. Sidewalk youth project has delivered detached youth work for over thirty years in Scarborough. There have been busy nights, and there have been silent nights! But consistency of delivery, where possible, has enhanced the sense of trust, visibility and a sense of dependability.

Ongoing Monitoring and Reporting

Recording and monitoring are important for a number of reasons. They measure progress, facilitate learning, identify follow-up actions and provide valuable reference information. It is worth considering how the team will engage in wider learning, based on information gathered. This may be done through meetings, training or supervision sessions. Records also provide evidence of outputs and outcomes for stakeholders. It is worthwhile planning how young people will contribute to the evaluative process too; developing youth-led work without young people's input will be tricky![42]

Moving on

Work may conclude for a number of reasons. Whatever they are, it is worth thinking through the process of ending well.

The work may have reached a natural conclusion, in which case, how do young people feed back, what are their next steps, and what will the organization do next?

Young people may have moved on, which may leave some work unresolved or unfinished. This is the nature of voluntary participation, and workers need to be prepared for this. It is worth bearing in mind that you may well connect with the group again at a later date, and the work done previously will have established foundations for any new engagement.

Funding may have ended or organizational changes may have resulted in winding up the project, which are causes beyond the control or say of young people. For this reason, it is important to consider how to end in a way that keeps young people informed. In centre-based projects, when a youth worker leaves, the resource of the centre remains. In detached work, when the workers leave, the resource is gone. Consider where and how young people might continue to access support. This may require referrals and introductions to other services where available.

When work with a group concludes, any learning and outcomes should be recorded and reflected on, to feed back to stakeholders and inform next steps.

6 Conclusion

We have reviewed the history and context of detached youth work, considered some theology and theory that informs the practice and outlined a process to implement. Now it is over to you!

Whilst unique in certain ways, detached youth work is essentially about adapting core youth work values to a specific context. It presents so many exciting possibilities. Communities can experience transformation when we resonate with and respond to the dynamic and creative nature of young people who bring alternative perspectives. Salvation comes from the margins. See you on the streets…

Notes

1 Michael Mather, *Having Nothing, Possessing Everything: Finding Abundant Communities in Unexpected Places* (Grand Rapids, MI: Eerdmans Publishing, 2018) p 4.

2 *ibid.*

3 J Sobrino, *No Salvation Outside the Poor: Prophetic-Utopian Essays* (Maryknoll, NY: Orbis, 2015).

4 G A Tiffany, *Reconnecting Detached Youth Work: Standards and Guidelines for Excellence* (Leicester: The Federation for Detached Youth Work, 2007) p 12.

5 J R Batsleer and B Davies, *What is Youth Work?* (Exeter: Learning Matters, 2010) p 57.

6 G A Tiffany, *op cit*, p 9.

7 'The Albemarle Report: activities and facilities,' infed.org, https://infed.org/mobi/the-albemarle-report-activities-and-facilities/ (accessed 15 April 2020).

8 See www.fyt.org.uk for details of resources and training.

9 G A Tiffany, *op cit*, p 6.

10 K Malone, 'Street life: youth, culture and competing uses of public space,' *Environment and Urbanization*, 14, 2002, p 158.

11 D Crimmens, F Factor, T Jeffs, J Pitts, C Pugh, J Spence and P Turner, *Reaching Socially Excluded Young People: A National Study of Street-based Youth Work* (Leicester: The National Youth Agency, 2004) p 14.

12 G A Tiffany, *op cit*, p 5.

13 *ibid.*

14 D Sibley, *Geographies of Exclusion* (London: Routledge, 1995).

15 G Bright, *Youth Work: Histories, Policy and Contexts* (London: Palgrave Macmillan, 2015) p 191.

16 Ken Worpole and Katharine Knox, *The Social Value Of Public Space* (York: Joseph Rowntree Foundation, 2007) p 2.

17 L H Doncaster, *God in Every Man* (London: Allen and Unwin, 1963) p 16.

18 J Ord (ed), *Critical Issues in Youth Work Management* (Abingdon: Routledge, 2013) p 74.

19 P Block, W Brueggemann and J McKnight, *An Other Kingdom: Departing the Consumer Culture* (Hoboken, NJ: Wiley, 2016) p 9.

20 Asset Based Community Development (ABCD), Nurture Development: www.nurturedevelopment.org/asset-based-community-development/ (accessed 15 April 2020).

21 K Malone, *op cit*, p 157.

22 K Malone, *op cit*, p 162.

23 Archbishop's Presidential Address, General Synod, York, July 2003: rowanwilliams.archbishopofcanterbury.org/articles.php/1826/archbishops-presidential-address-general-synod-york-july-2003 (accessed 15 April 2020).

24 P Freire, *Pedagogy of the Oppressed* (New York: Continuum, 2000) p 80.

25 L H Doncaster, *op cit*, p 53.

26 *ibid*, p 16.

27 R Rohr, *Adam's Return: The Five Promises of Male Initiation* (New York: Crossroad Pub, 2004) p 136.

28 V Turner, *Betwixt-and-Between: The Liminal Period in Rites de Passage. In the Forest of Symbols: Aspects of Ndembu Ritual* (Ithaca, NY: Cornell University Press, 1967).

29 S H Lee, *From a Liminal Place: An Asian American Theology* (Minneapolis, MN: Augsburg Fortress Press, 2010).

30 V Turner, *The Ritual Process: Structure and Anti-Stru*cture (New York: Aldine Transaction, 1996) p 98.

31 B D Anshiso, *Jesus's Identification with the Marginalized and the Liminal: The Messianic Identity in Mark* (Carlisle: Langham Publishing, 2018) p 16.

32 G A Tiffany, *op cit*, p 7.

33 V Turner, *The Ritual Process: Structure and Anti-Structure* (New York: Aldine Transaction, 1996) p 94.

34 M Buber, *I and Thou* (London: Continuum, London) p 17.

35 Federation for Detached Youth Work (ed), *Detached Youth Work: Guidelines*. (Leicester: Federation for Detached Youth Work, 2007) p 17.

36 For guidance see https://www.cutr.usf.edu/oldpubs/CIA/Chapter_4.pdf

37 R Passmore, L Passmore and J Ballantyne, *Here be Dragons: Youth Work and Mission off the Map* (London: Frontier Youth Trust, 2013).

38 G A Tiffany, *op cit*, p 28.

39 *ibid*.

40 S Bevans, *Prophetic Dialogue : Reflections on Christian Mission Today* (Maryknoll, NY: Orbis Books, 2011) p 32.

41 #ThinkingThursdays | The Fire that Wouldn't Go Out, Frontier Youth Trust, 2019: www.fyt.org.uk/blog/blogs/thinkingthursdays-the-fire-that-wouldnt-go-out/ (accessed 16 April 2020).

42 See www.youthworkessentials.org/media/51546/measuring_outcomes_lres.pdf for guidance.